the library of african american arts and culture

rap and hip hop

The voice of a generation

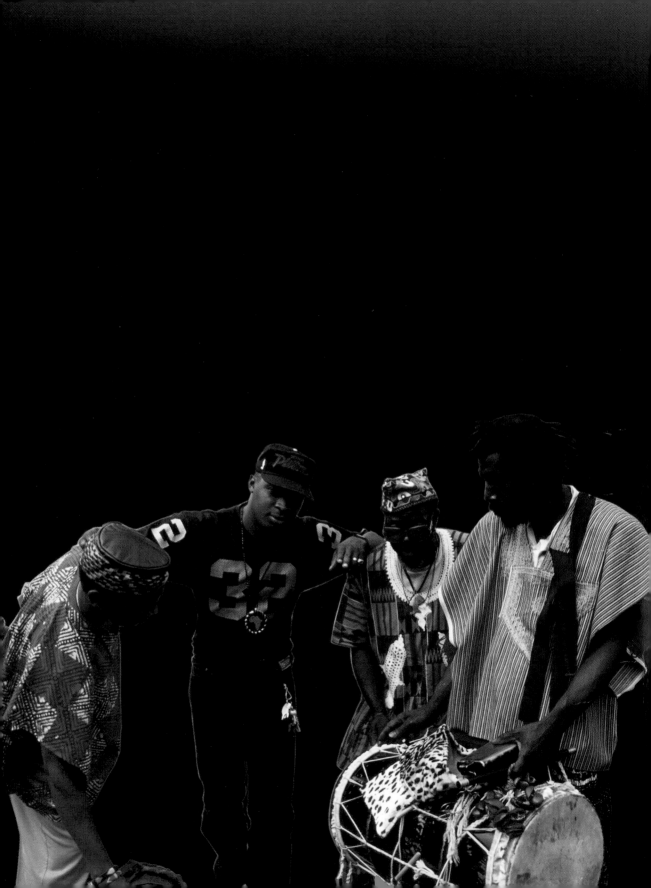

the library of african american arts and culture

rap and hip hop

The voice of a generation

sherry ayazi-hashjin

rosen publishing group, inc./new york

Published in 1999 by The Rosen Publishing Group, Inc.
29 East 21st Street, New York, NY 10010

Copyright © 1999 by The Rosen Publishing Group, Inc.

First Edition

Library of Congress Cataloging-in-Publication Data

Ayazi-Hashjin, S.
   Rap and hip hop : the voice of a generation / Sherry Ayazi-Hashjin.
      p. cm. —(The library of African American arts and culture)
   Includes bibliographical references and index.
   Summary : Describes the art of rapping and the cultural phenomenon
of hip hop, tracing its evolution from African and Caribbean traditions.
   ISBN 0-8239-1855-6
   1. Rap (Music)—History and criticism. 2. Hip-hop—United States.
  [1. Rap (Music) 2. Hip-hop.] I. Title. II. Series.
ML3531.A93 1999
782.421649—dc21
                                    99-10972
                                         CIP
                                         AC

Contents

Introduction

This book is the story of the journey of an art form known as rap and a cultural phenomenon called hip hop. Within this story you will learn about many musical styles and about youth, innovation, and inspiration. Hip hop is about heritage, identity, and the future.

Hip hop includes not only rapping, but also DJing, breakdancing, and graffiti art. These arts have traveled a long way through time. Though hip hop is considered a recent cultural development, its roots stretch back to before Columbus's voyage to the New World.

In this book we unfold the layers which make up the art form of rap. We will also see how hip hop culture takes lessons from its African heritage.

The modern urban lifestyle of hip hop was born in New York City in the early 1970s. Through the art of rapping, African American youth documented what was going on around them and what they thought about it. Rap also reminds listeners of the cultures—African and African American—from which it springs.

For any "hip hop head," an exciting hip hop track can give you goosebumps. The infectious beat of rap music, with the aid of both technology and imagination, drives a cut-and-mix formula of composing. The sounds invite you to nod your head in frenzied enjoyment. You'll rewind and play a chosen track until you memorize every verse of your favorite MC's rhymes.

Hip hop had its beginnings as an underground sound: Only a few people took part in its creation, and at first, only a few enjoyed it. However, that is no longer the case. Hip hop is always evolving, and new styles are constantly created through freestyling and DJing. Rap music's audience is still growing and is continually awaiting the next new hip hop release.

Rap is finally being recognized as a key part of the history of African American music. Chuck D, rapper and producing member of the group Public Enemy, calls rap "Black America's CNN" and the "Black American folktale." Rap is a commentary, an opinion about the events of our time. MCs (mic controllers/masters of ceremony) are both broadcasters and poets, representing urban youth.

Hip hop is an educational resource. Through the language of music, it is teaching listeners the world over about modern culture.

Family

Rap is a young member of a long and distinguished musical family tree. Its forebears paved the way for past and future hip hop generations.

The godfathers of rap are pioneering MCs such as the Furious Five, The Fantastic Five, Afrika Bambaataa & The SoulSonic Force, and the Treacherous Three. They began to rhyme lyrics for fun as their DJs—Grandmaster Flash, Grand Wizard Theodore, DJ Kool Herc, Jazzy Jay, and DJ Breakout—experimented with the controlled scratching and mixing of records. Some people gave themselves names like "Crazy Legs," "Doze," and "Freeze," and they did a dance known as "breaking" to this liberating new beat.

The grandfathers of hip hop are poets and musicians such as Gil Scott-Heron, The Last Poets, Langston Hughes, and the Watts Prophets.

Its teachers—revolutionary blues, jazz, and funk musicians—are alive and kicking on the vinyl LPs found on the turntables of today's greatest DJs. Hip hop caused a resurgence of public interest in the music of artists such as James Brown, Miles Davis, Rare Earth, The Ohio Players, and Roy Ayers.

Hip hop's cousins are ska, rocksteady, reggae, and dancehall music, born to distant musical uncles and aunts in Jamaica and the West Indies. The earlier forms had come to the New World from Nigeria, Senegal, the Guinea Coast, and the Congo.

Always Changing

Hip hop is more popular now than it has ever been. It has gone through many changes since its early days, but its roots are still alive.

Even now, while riding on the New York City subway, you can still catch a glimpse of lit-up tunnels that bear pictures, called "tags" or "pieces," of graffiti artists. In the 1970s these artists were superstars of a fresh young scene. Since then, graffiti has moved to new canvases, but it is still influencing generations of artists. Today the cardboard taped down on the sidewalk on which kids practiced new breakdancing "freezes" is no longer in sight. But breaking is still taught by its pioneers. Kids are still rhyming on street corners. They're performing their own brand of street poetry.

Hip hop is its own culture, and rap is its oratory. It is a modern expression of an ancient tradition, helping to keep a rich cultural history alive.

Yo, hip hop is a way of life. It ain't a fad. It ain't a trend. Not for those of us who are true to it ... It's our way to release tension, to let out the frustration that young people face in the world today. Over the years hip hop has evolved to represent what is happening now—the reality of street life. Rap is the oral expression of this. The tool, the literature ... it will still remain for some of us the raw essence of life. Peace.

—rapper/producer Guru

12

1 heritage

Africa, the second-largest continent in the world, is more than three times the size of the United States. It consists of fifty-three countries and at least 500 million people. Africa is home to many different ethnic groups and cultures, all with their own languages, traditions, and religions.

Although Africa contains many separate nations, there are strong forces that bond the peoples of this land together. The African musical tradition is one of these forces.

The Musical Tradition

In Africa the playing of music is not simply a recreational activity. Music complements the rhythm of life. African musicians aim to create music that expresses life in all of its aspects.

In Africa, music and dance are not just entertainment—they are a way of life.

To record the history of hip hop, we must break down the two most important elements of its heritage: the drum and the griot. The drum symbolizes the heartbeat. The griot is a storyteller who builds a story against the backdrop of the drum.

I sing: I think
-Zairean song lyric

The Drum

In Africa the drum has been a vital tool of communication for centuries. The sound of the drum is also reflected in the form of hand clapping, stamping, or rhythmic beating of objects such as the pestle and mortar.

The sounds of instruments in Africa are considered humanlike: They are referred to as voices. These sounds are seen as an extension of the drummer and not as a separate tool or object.

Both in the past and in modern-day Africa, the drum is considered sacred. The Ashanti people of West Africa believe that there is a man on the moon who is a drummer. Others believe that God speaks through the sound of the drum. The player of the talking drum is thought to be close to the essence of nature. He is known as the Creator's Drummer. When he plays, he

Drums are the heartbeat of the song and are the heartbeat of the spirit, too . . . that's where the real subliminal message comes from.

—rapper / producer
True Master

15

reproduces the patterns and sounds of speech.

In the 1970s the pioneers of hip hop recreated the drum. Instead of being carved out of wood and covered in animal skins, it took the form of turntables. Today's DJ is an urban drummer, recreating the drum-heartbeat by mixing and scratching sounds and voices from old records and mixing beats electronically on drum machines.

types of drums:

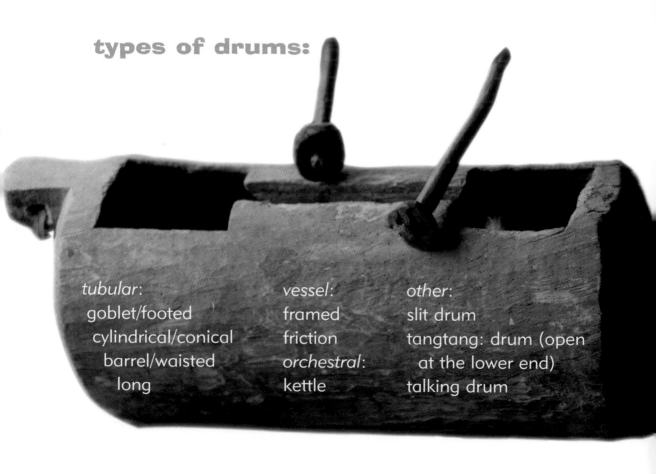

tubular:
goblet/footed
cylindrical/conical
barrel/waisted
long

vessel:
framed
friction
orchestral:
kettle

other:
slit drum
tangtang: drum (open
   at the lower end)
talking drum

In Jamaica people have taken African influences to make their own special kind of music, which is like a cousin to American hip hop.

... deep rooted is my rhymin' /
like ancient African griots /
precise is my timin' ...

-rapper/producer Guru

The Griot

The griot is the name given to members of West African society who know and tell stories, both historical and imaginary, to their communities. They convey lessons through music, song, memory, and ancestral wisdom. In America, hip hop artists maintain many of these same roles in the eyes of their fans. MCs speak to their listeners in a style similar to that of the African ancestral tradition, although they speak a different language to another kind of beat.

Rap records tell today's story in a language we can relate to. We turn to the talents of the RZA of the Wu-Tang Clan, KRS-One, and Tupac Shakur for words to remind us that we are not alone.

Song Types

Today African influences are found in many kinds of music. Two African song types—the holler and call-and-response—played an important role in the development of many kinds of African American music, including hip hop. The holler, also called the field holler or falsetto break, is one song type found in

Tupac Shakur

African music. It is made up of one musical verse, often sung over and over. It sounds like a kind of yell or cry. The holler sound includes calling, wailing, humming, rasping, growling, wavering, whining, and bending. Often hollers were sung as people worked outside, as a way to communicate with one another.

The influence of the field holler can be found in later music, in the form of a break. In blues and jazz, a musician will break away from the melody and create fill-in music by improvising. In hip hop, DJs create breaks by scratching. MCs call out to the audience in the same manner with an "uh, and you don't stop" or a "rock, rock on."

Call-and-response is another African song type. This style of music resembles the rhythm of conversation: One person speaks; the other answers. This can occur between singers, between instruments, or between a singer and an instrument.

Call-and-response can be found in spirituals when the preacher speaks and the congregation responds with cries of "Hallelujah," or "Wake 'em up, brudder." It is also used in blues and jazz when a singer calls out a "yes, man" or a "play it" and the musician plays. In this case the singer calls, and

Rapper Ice Cube listens to his audience respond.

the music responds.

In his song "Say It Loud," soul singer James Brown uses call-and-response as he calls out,

SAY IT LOUD . . .

and his backup singers respond,

. . . I'M BLACK AND I'M PROUD.

Passage

African music has inspired many generations of African Americans. However, these traditions have had a difficult journey. They were brought to America when Africans were forced to come to the New World as slaves.

From the 1500s into the 1800s, people from western and central Africa were captured and transported against their will to the West Indies and the thirteen colonies. Many slaves worked on the large farms, called plantations, in the American South. Slavery was a huge business and made many white Americans rich, but the conditions that African Americans suffered were unbelievably cruel.

An estimated 10 to 15 million people crossed the Atlantic packed into unsanitary slave ships. The route these ships took is known as the Middle Passage. Many people died on this terrible journey. Others survived only to be separated from their families, sold, and forced to do hard labor for the rest of their lives. Slaves were considered property, not human beings.

Africans who were brought to America found themselves living in a strange land with unfamiliar customs, religions, and languages. These first generations of African Americans were forbidden to follow their own traditions. Activities such as dances and religious rituals, which brought the slaves together and reinforced their African identity, were outlawed. Because of a slave rebellion, known as the Cato Conspiracy, the drum was

outlawed too. During this rebellion a group of escaped slaves, lead by a slave named Cato, used drums to communicate with African Americans on neighboring plantations. As a result, in 1740 slave owners throughout the South banned drums, fearing more rebellions.

Despite these circumstances, however, African Americans kept the spirit alive. They could not write their new history down, but they preserved it for centuries through oral culture—by "telling it how it was" to one another. Although the drum was outlawed, slaves on large plantations who could not be closely monitored continued to use drums, while others came up with new ways to make music. These traditions and innovations were passed on from one generation to the next and have maintained a proud heritage.

We are linked in both life and death. Those who share common blood relations never break apart.
—Tom Feelings, *The Middle Passage*

2 musical roots

To understand rap, it is important to know about all the styles of African American music that came before it. Just as hip hop began underground, so did many other kinds of music. As these early styles became more popular, they paved the way for hip hop culture.

Spirituals

The spiritual is a kind of African American religious folk song that was born during the era of slavery and grew up in the years after emancipation. Many African Americans adopted Christianity during this time.

But they created their own form of Christian worship according to their traditions. They sang Christian hymns but added their own style and often their own words.

African American slaves could identify with the teachings of the Bible—many saw biblical connections with the obstacles in their own lives. The Old and New Testaments describe spiritual trials, triumphs over oppression, and teachings of endurance. When rappers talk about overcoming hardship and finding freedom, they refer to the tradition of spirituals.

Blues

The blues was born in the beginning of the twentieth century. In the years earlier—specifically after the Civil War ended in 1865—African Americans had been freed from slavery. They began to settle in different parts of the United States, and the music that they played started to change.

Blues music developed from many different

In blues music, African Americans began to sing of worldly concerns rather than religious matters.

traditions—African song types, including call-and-response and holler; spirituals; and ballads about adventuresome heroes and infamous outlaws. Yet the blues took on subjects that were entirely new. Blues music was concerned with loss, loneliness, and taboo subjects such as drinking and gambling.

Blues has contributed to hip hop in many ways. One is its attitude. Although the subject matter of the blues is fears, woes, hard luck, and love (often lost), the musicians and singers often express their feelings in a clever and humorous way, as rappers do.

The musical structure of blues also influenced hip hop. Blues players' use of riffs—single rhythmic phrases repeated over and over as background to (or part of) the melody—is an early version of the booming bass line of many hip hop tracks.

Blues also contributed to hip hop once the blues evolved into the more extravagant, electric-sounding funk, which is widely sampled by hip hop DJs.

Bessie Smith, "the Empress of the Blues"

Jazz

Jazz was born in the early part of this century. One of the very first places jazz was performed regularly was New Orleans. Small ensembles of brass and wind instruments played lively, improvised music that had surprising offbeats and interwoven rhythms.

Soon jazz took root in cities such as Chicago and New York, and then it swept the country. It evolved into new styles such as big band and swing, played by small orchestras. These orchestras relied mostly on written music instead of improvisation, since jazz was being recorded and played on the radio and needed to hold to a strict time schedule.

In the 1940s another style of jazz, called bebop, emerged. A handful of musicians were looking to create something new. They started playing unpredictable melodies, complex rhythms, and new tones. If you say the word "bebop" out loud, you can get a sense of the irregular, changing accents in bebop music. Bebop brought revolution into jazz, and soon this style rose to acclaim.

Later styles of jazz, such

Louis "Satchmo" Armstrong

as free jazz and fusion, drew from African roots. At the same time, artists were also tapping into new sounds and technology. A hip hop sensibility began to emerge. In the 1970s, jazz fusion singer and musician Gil Scott-Heron performed powerful rap poems such as "Small Talk on 125th and Lennox," "No Knock," and "H_2Ogate Blues."

The Harlem Renaissance

Jazz music played a major part in the Harlem Renaissance, one of the great intellectual movements of this century.

Based in the New York City neighborhood of Harlem, the Harlem Renaissance presented itself in fresh, forward-thinking forms of literature, art, and music that portrayed the experiences of African Americans.

Jazz thrived in this atmosphere. This was a time when New York nightclubs such as The Cotton Club and Connie's Inn were popular jazz spots.

The Harlem Renaissance left a permanent mark on American culture. Black art and intellect received respect that it had not had before. The door was now open for new forms of expression to develop.

Fifty years later, hip hop culture emerged north of Harlem in the neighborhood of the South Bronx, addressing many of the same concerns as the Harlem Renaissance.

The poet Langston Hughes is one of the most celebrated artists of the Harlem Renaissance

Gil Scott-Heron comments on being a forefather of rap:

I'm glad they use me. They're doing their own thing, but I keep telling [rappers] that if they look to me they should know of my influences too. By using me, they use them.

Cousins: The Jamaican Inspiration

Jamaican music and hip hop can be described as musical cousins. You may have heard the unquestionable power of a Jamaican rastaman's chant. Bob Marley played internationally popular roots reggae, which was born of a people's unrest. He has been referred to as a prophet, spreading the message of peace.

However, even before roots reggae became popular,

an underground form of Jamaican music was brewing. Its language was direct and spoken in broken English or patois. "Signifying" and "toasting" were the names given to a more modern form of storytelling in the Caribbean tradition that included rhyming and simple tale-telling, boasting, and inventing humorous insults. The "deejay"—the Jamaican predecessor to the American MC—was the performer. This form of rap was also called "chanting 'pon the mike."

Dances were organized nightly during the '50s, '60s, and '70s. The music the deejays played varied, but as the style of deejaying evolved, they began to play "dub" tracks, instrumentals, or B-sides of a song. This provided a backdrop for the deejay to toast over.

The sound system used to play this music included a turntable, an amplifier, and enormous speakers. There were many sound systems during this time, and each was given its own name. The most legendary of

Bob Marley

these included Dicky's Dynamic, Sir George Atomic, Coxsone's Downbeat, and King Tubby's Hometown Hi-Fi. While a "selector" was responsible for playing the records, the deejay announced the tracks.

Jamaican deejays such as Count Machouki, Sir Lord Comic, U Roy (also known as the Originator), King Stitt, and I Roy toasted over what they described as "riddims," using phrases such as "Live the life you love and love the life you live," "Wake the town and tell the people," "This station rule the nation with version," and scats like "chick-a-bow-wow-wow." Nowadays artists such as Yellowman, SuperCat, Shabba Ranks, Buju Banton, and Beenie Man follow the same Jamaican deejay tradition while also collaborating with hip hop artists.

The Originators

Although hip hop has many inspirations, it was truly born when a few people used their skills and imagination to create a brand-new sound.

DJ Kool Herc

Clive Campbell, aka DJ Kool Herc, is the man responsible for importing the concept of "deejaying" from Jamaica to America. He moved to New York from Kingston, Jamaica, at twelve years of age, in 1967. Later he originated hip hop's version of rapping based on the art of Jamaican "toasting."

By 1974 Herc had built his own sound system, including huge speakers that he called "the Herculords." Instead of playing Jamaican music, Kool Herc played popular American music: James

Brown and Rare Earth. He would shout out to the audience with lines such as:

Yes yes y'all. It's the serious, serio-so jointski You're listening to the sound system: The Herculords . . . culords . . . lords and I just want to say to all my B-boys . . . boys . . . oys . . . Rock on!

It was DJ Kool Herc who gave breakdancers their name. For a time he "spun the tracks" and also performed as an MC. But soon he began to employ other kids to MC while he concentrated on controlling the turntables, or "wheels of steel." Many people credit Kool Herc's Coke La Rock as the very first MC. While Kool Herc mastered the new art of playing break beats manually on his turntables, Coke La Rock would control the microphone and entertain the audience.

Kool Herc brought break beat music to rap. He would create a break by sampling parts of a track and playing them over and over again. Whereas machines were used for sampling later on in rap's history, Kool Herc accomplished all of this by hand.

Afrika Bambaataa

When high school student Kevin Donovan, who had been a member of a Bronx street gang known as the Black Spades, heard Kool Herc's collection of songs, he delved into the enormous stack of records he and his mother had at home. He decided to start his own sound system when his mother bought him two turntables as a graduation gift. He called himself Afrika Bambaataa, meaning "affectionate leader," and was later known as Master of Records due to the vast variety of music he sampled.

Bambaataa played the sounds of James Brown, the Rolling Stones, and the Herman Kelly Band at his first party in November 1976 at the Bronx River Community Center. With musical interests ranging from African, calypso, and classical music to the rock of The Who and Led Zeppelin, and inspiration from the teachings of the Black Panthers, NAACP, Malcolm X, and Martin Luther King Jr., Bambaataa left his days as a gangster behind. He built his own positive youth group. First named The Organization and later renamed the Zulu Nation, it is still in effect today.

33

Grandmaster Flash

As more and more sound systems started to appear, DJs would battle it out on the turntables (often while their MCs would do the same on the mic) at parks and community centers.

Joseph Saddler, a high school electronics major, decided to join the battle of the New York sound systems. Now he is better known as Grandmaster Flash. He developed a skillful technique called backspinning as a way to create a break.

He accomplished this by discovering the uses of the SPDT (single-pole, double-throw) switch, also known as a toggle or clip switch. When he found a disco DJ using this switch on his mixer to cue the next track through his headphones, Grandmaster Flash installed one on his own mixer. By using two copies of the same record and playing each one on a separate turntable, he would cut back and forth using the SPDT switch to make the desired break. With a pair of headphones, he was able to simultaneously cue the record back, allowing the break to last for several minutes.

While Herc and others were dropping their turntable needles on records and randomly finding a beat to play, Flash used this more controlled style to become the top DJ in the Bronx.

Grand Wizard Theodore

Grandmaster Flash had a partner at this time called Mean Gene. They would send Mean Gene's little brother out to buy records for them. Although Mean Gene's younger brother didn't DJ yet, he secretly practiced on the turntables at home. Later he became known as Grand Wizard Theodore.

Theodore accidentally discovered a new technique in his room one day. His mother was shouting at him for playing the music too loud, and when she opened the door to his room, he stopped the record with his finger while the turntable was still spinning. In his headphones he could hear the needle scratching the record. He liked the sound and realized he could use it to create a new kind of break.

Theodore's discovery at the age of thirteen was scratching: moving a record back and forth on a turntable and letting the needle scratch on the groove. Soon every DJ started to use this innovative addition to the sound they were calling hip hop.

Respect
the Architect

Sampling began because kids didn't have the money to buy instruments, so they found them on already-made tracks.

Even though some critics think of sampling as stealing, others see it as the complex technique of transforming something old into something completely new by taking a snippet of a song and altering it. Parliament Funkadelic star George Clinton, the second most sampled artist next to James Brown, refers to being sampled as simply a part of keeping the funk alive. Hip hop has brought back the music of artists who had been temporarily forgotten.

DJs go to great lengths to protect the source of the samples they use in their break beats, because the ones they discover become their signature tracks. Deejays in Jamaica as well as Kool Herc used to soak away the labels on their vinyl records in water so as not

Types of scratches and turntable wizardry include:

the baby or wikki wikki,
the cut or forward scratch,
the transformer,
beat juggling or chasing,
military scratch,
the tweak,
the flare.

to give away the names of the tracks they had chosen to play. Afrika Bambaataa would cross off or tape over the titles on the labels of his records.

The hip hop DJ is not simply a disc jockey but a type of musician. DJs are the architects of the hip hop sound.

Check the Technique

When rap began, it was the DJ who called out to the audience between scratching or breaking. DJs like Kool Herc were creative and entertaining in the way that they called out songs. The early DJs were actually the first hip hop MCs.

As new technology developed, however, the DJ role changed. Samplers and drum machines helped open more doors into the realm of new beats. Digital sampling allowed the DJ to extract a particular beat or catchy melody from an old song and then "loop" it electronically, so it would repeat over and over. Drum machines let DJs add a new rhythmic layer to a loop. As a result, DJs are

I don't think DJing can ever die out because it started rap, yunno. DJing is rap.

-DJ Sean C

now more like composers and producers than live instrumentalists.

Few DJs use the original setup when performing live. Most play the instrumental track from a DAT (digital audiotape) with everything, including scratches and

Gang Starr

breaks, previously recorded. In the live performance, the MC rhymes over these recorded beats. However, there are still DJs who maintain their position behind the turntables.

Gang Starr's DJ Premier is an example of a DJ who still performs live but also uses prerecorded beats. The group presses instrumentals of their tracks on vinyl for DJ Premier to perform with while Guru, the MC of the duo, rhymes at live performances. DJ competitions, such as the Battle for World Supremacy Championship and the USA/World DMC Championship, focus on battling on the turntables the way the early DJs did with their huge sound systems during the '70s.

DJing crews like the X-Men still dedicate themselves

Another instrument or sonic backdrop for the rapper is the sounds of the "Human Beat Box". The voice can make the music while the rapper rhymes.

Doug E Fresh, Biz Markie, and the Fat Boys' Darren Robinson are pioneering examples of men who used their vocal chords and lips to create percussion. Their tongue clicks, gurgles, hums, and grunts are similar to the m'bira players in Zimbabwe, the Bushmen of the Kalahari Desert, and the pygmies of central Africa.

to pushing the boundaries of scratching and mixing. These crews are made up of stars such as Rob Swift, Sinister, Sean C, and Roc Raider, whose influences were pioneering DJs like Grandmaster Flash, Charlie Chase, Grandmixer D.ST., Cash Money, and Aladdin.

The Changing Sound

The DJs responsible for the changing sound are those who continue to explore new melodies and rhythms. They use them to create tracks that stand out from the rest.

Key innovators with signature sounds follow in the footsteps of those such as Marley Marl, DJ Mark the 45 King, Pete Rock, Diamond D, Large Professor, and Lord Finesse. These producers have made some of hip hop's classic tracks. Another producer who has earned respect with his diverse skills is Prince Paul, who has been a part of rap since the early 1980s, when he was in the group Stetsasonic. He produced the original sound of the group De La Soul and later became a member of the Gravediggaz.

Another East Coast-based

DJ/producer is DJ Premier. He is a member of the long-standing duo known as Gang Starr. He has contributed to classic albums of such rappers as the Notorious B.I.G., Jeru the Damaja, KRS-One, and MOP while branching off to work with jazz musicians such as Branford Marsalis.

The RZA emerged out of Staten Island and onto the hip hop scene with a diverse group of rappers who call themselves the Wu-Tang Clan. The RZA has produced solo albums for Wu-Tang members GZA, ODB, Raekwon the Chef, Cappadonna, and Ghostface and has launched his own solo career.

The Notorious B.I.G.

The Bomb Squad, comprised of Long Island-based producers Eric "Vietnam" Sadler, Keith and Hank Shocklee, and Chuck D, formed the rap group Public Enemy. Not only was PE's sound innovative, but they were early creators of a positive, outspoken, original political message. They have also collaborated with rappers like Slick Rick and Ice Cube and R&B artists such as Bell Biv Devoe and Vanessa Williams.

West coast rapper and producer Dr Dre began his

the music and hear the dance."

Likewise, while MCs were busy dueling on the mic, a simultaneous battle began on the dance floor.

B-boys break-danced. (The *B* in B-boy stands for "break.") B-boys would invent new moves known as "freezes." The freezes were given names such as "the baby," "the dead," "the turtle," "the back bridge," "the headache," "the back spin," and "the head spin." B-boys would tape cardboard down onto the street and practice their moves on this smooth surface.

At parties the B-boys would show off their skills. Crews such as Starchild La Rock, New York City Breakers, Rockwell Association, Dynamic Rockers, and the well-known Rock Steady Crew, who are still growing in numbers worldwide, held competitions against one another.

Members of the Rock Steady Crew such as Crazy Legs, Doze, Rasean, Ken Swift, Frosty Freeze, Joe Joe,

Take 1, Mr. Freeze, Lenny Len, Ken Roc, Ty Fly, and Kippy Dee each had their own original styles of breakin'. As with MCing, B-boys started breakdancing just for fun, but they wound up inventing a brand new competitive sport.

By 1983, B-boys found themselves on the covers of magazines and newspapers and featured in movies such as *Flashdance* and *Beat Street*. The documentary film *Style Wars* records their exploits alongside those of graffiti artists. Break dancers moved rapidly from their raw beginnings within the underground hip hop culture to international acclaim.

Crazy Legs still teaches B-boyin' classes at Point Community Center in the Bronx, New York, and is featured in new hip hop music videos. The Rock Steady Crew holds reunions every year in New York City, and the Break Dance Championships take place worldwide.

Painting a Picture Never to Be Forgotten

In New York City, when underground subway tunnels momentarily light up as a train passes through them, you can see the work of graffiti artists.

By 1973 graffiti was being noticed

on the New York subway systems. Each artist had an alias. Individuals who went by the names of Taki 183, Super Kool 223, Lee 163d, Phase 2, Tracy 168, Papo 184, Stitch I, and Barbara and Eva 62 paved the way, and graffiti caught on. The works of art they produced were called "tags," "pieces," or "burners."

With phenomenal artistry, graffiti writers competed to make their names known and recognized by their peers on the subway systems of New York City. As with breakdancing, DJing, and MCing, graffiti had its stars such as Crash, Daze, Dondi, Skeme, Kase 2, and Seen.

However, in the 1980s New York City's mayor, Edward Koch, waged a war against graffiti art on the subway systems. Subway cars today are made of a metal on which paint will not stick. The last train that could be painted on was taken out of service in 1989. But graffiti found other mediums, from neighborhood murals to upscale art galleries.

Today, if you look around the world, you will find hip hop graffiti art. Young people still "tag," and they keep sketchbooks and albums documenting their pieces. The literal "writing on the wall" continues to be a cutting edge means of artistic and poetic expression.

5 lyrical: the mc

The rap arena, like that of any sport, is highly competitive. A rapper must work hard at his or her skill in order to gain recognition and respect. As with boxing, skill will crush the weak. Like the martial arts, a lack of skill exposes those not true to the form. As in the game of chess, only time can tell who will outwit his opponent and achieve longevity under the spotlight.

Missy "Misdemeanor" Elliott

Freestyling

Freestyling is to an MC what soloing is to a jazz musician. It's more than just rhyming off the top of your head. Freestyling is a difficult skill. It combines the elements of beat and lyricism. Some say that it defines the difference between just a rapper and an MC. An MC has a message and works to get across an idea in an original way.

When hip hop began, there was nothing but freestyling. Rappers would get up on stage and say

It is scary to freestyle, to risk making a mistake in front of others, but MCs just go for it. By just showing the effort to try, it shows that you're committed to all facets of the music form, not just the ones that earn the ducats.

-rapper T-Love

whatever came into their heads. No one had a record deal. They were doing it simply because they loved to.

Rhyming began to take off with the early microphone skills of Busy Bee, Starski the Lovebug, Melle Mel (of Grandmaster Flash's Furious Five), Grand Wizard Theodore's Fantastic Five, DJ Breakout's Funky Four + One More, and the Treacherous Three. Crews of MCs, backed by their trusted DJs, would compete against one another in the parks and anywhere else they could find. Talented young men and women would show off their skills at breaking, mixing, and rhyming.

The scene was buzzing with a freshness that was bound to catch on. As this sound began to emerge from the underground, people took notice.

In 1979 Sylvia Robinson of Sugar Hill Records was responsible for signing The Sugar Hill Gang and releasing on vinyl their anthem "Rapper's Delight." The song became a disco favorite, using the styles of hip hop's originators. Its worldwide success gave the mainstream a taste of this new art form. Sugar Hill Records became the home to hip hop greats and was followed by independent record labels such as Enjoy, UNI, Tuff City, B Boy, and Def Jam.

From the early 1980s on, people of all cultures and tastes began to catch hip hop's buzz. Hip hop became a part of fashion and popular culture across the United States and around the world.

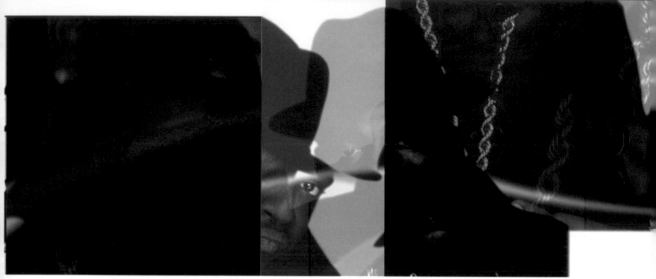

Lessons

Most rap tunes being made in the early 1980s were
fun boasts and "disses" that were made for partying.
But soon many rappers began to speak of their lives as
urban kids. The harsh conditions of the mind, soul,
and body that many young African Americans dealt
with daily became a subject of discussion.

Rappers have used their art as a way to resist and
criticize these conditions. At times, harsh realities have
been documented with harsh words. In the late 1980s
the rapping of DJ Polo and Kool G Rap, NWA, X-Clan,
Boogie Down Productions, and Gang Starr took on
subjects of violence and anger.

Because the subjects were controversial, they resulted
in a lot of criticism of rap. However, many of the artists
who graphically depict violence in their lyrics argue that
the intention is not to glorify acts of violence but to
speak of reality to an audience who can relate.

The rap group Public Enemy, with Chuck D rapping alongside Flavor Flav and the varied tones of DJ Terminator X, released important albums like *It Takes a Nation of Millions to Hold Us Back* (1988) and *Fear of a Black Planet* (1990). PE is one of the definitive voices of "knowledgeable rap," verbally confronting institutional racism, police corruption, and the legacy of slavery in the United States.

A Tribe Called Quest

Urban society is not bound by the laws of ethnic culture. And urban music is an expression of this society.

-Ashenafi Kebede

Since then, other rappers have promoted positive messages. For example, with songs like "Stop the Violence" and "Self-Destruction," KRS-One has dedicated his talent to opening the ears of a world that often seems cruel and drenched in hate. Eric B and Rakim, EPMD, Schoolly D, Slick Rick, Poor Righteous Teachers, and Ice Cube all helped build this movement.

The 1990s have seen many styles of rap. Each group or solo rapper has a distinct message and sound, whether it be the storytelling of Slick Rick or the uplifting Nation of Islam-inspired tracks by Brand Nubian on their album *In God We Trust*. The X-Clan, Jungle Brothers, Queen Latifah, A Tribe Called Quest, De La Soul, and Lauryn Hill have all contributed to hip hop music with complex, literate, and powerful rhymes that make a point of showing respect toward the African motherland. The power of music has allowed a journey of inspiration and enlightenment to be shared by the youth who listen.

Queen Latifah

6 looking ahead

Interlude

People who criticize rap have said that it's not really music. Some think that "music" can only be played with traditional musical instruments and traditional singing styles. Some argue that rap is offensive to the ear and that its message is violent and negative.

Then there are critics within the hip hop community who argue that rap music was once a true art form but

Wyclef Jean

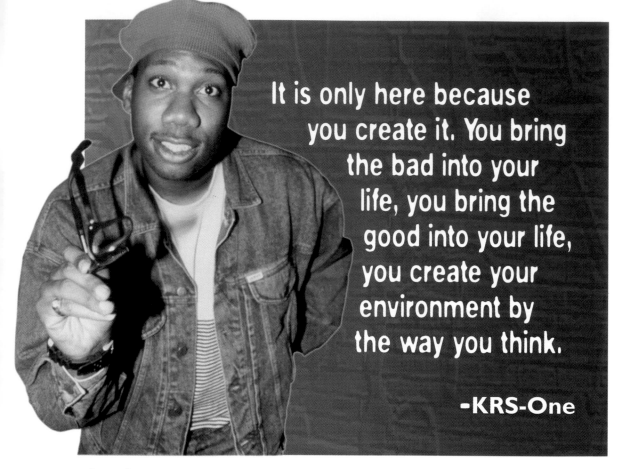

> It is only here because you create it. You bring the bad into your life, you bring the good into your life, you create your environment by the way you think.
>
> **-KRS-One**

has become corrupted by money. They say hip hop died when it became popular and that now rap is nothing but a commodity. There are those who say hip hop was better in the days when MCs, DJs, B-boys, and graffiti artists were just out there to have fun, not to make money.

Throughout the years, rap has been dismissed by all kinds of people for all kinds of reasons. However, it has always carried righteous messages for those who were willing to listen carefully. As more and more people opened their ears, more records sold. In fact, it can be argued that the widespread commercial success of hip hop artists proves what a powerful art form it is, and that rap's presence in mainstream culture is a victory for African Americans.

Hip hop was once a form of underground entertainment. From the start, rap has told raw, expressive, and controversial stories. We must not forget why this art form emerged in the first place: Youth needed to express themselves. They had something important to say.

Lauryn Hill

The untimely deaths of rappers Eazy E, KRS-One's DJ Scott LaRock, Tupac Shakur, and the Notorious B.I.G. tell us that today's reality needs to change. The hip hop community will deal with these harsh realities as it has always done. It will challenge the ways of thinking and

The thing that frightened people about hip hop was that they heard people enjoying the rhythm for rhythm's sake. Hip hop lives in the world—not the world of music—that's why it is so revolutionary.
•Max Roach

the ignorance that lead to these tragedies by "telling it like it is" and telling us how it could be. Like the griots of African tradition, MCs will continue to offer us lessons to be heard.

Rappers and DJs who stay true to the art form are keeping the beat alive. They will argue, with their "show and prove" skills, that hip hop is alive and well. Not only rhymes but beats will evolve and change. The DJs of the future will have new technology and new techniques. There will be new collaborations with other kinds of musicians, new ways of making hip hop tracks, and new ways to think about them.

Hip hop is a form of expression created by young people. Its roots can be traced back to Africa, but it is also an art form focused on the future. It teaches us to strive for newness not only through the medium of sound but through the way we learn, create, and live our lives.

As I sit by my window in Brooklyn, New York, I hear the sounds of my surrounding reality. Jeeps roll by pumping the music of Fat Joe, Big Pun, Group Home, and other stars of our time. I see kids hanging out on their stoops during the hot summer months when school is out. Like the founders of hip hop, they are showing off their rhyme skills. I know hip hop is here to stay.

ballad   A traditional kind of song that tells a story.

break beats   A point in hip hop music when there is a stop or abrupt change in the song and a new beat or riff is inserted.

breaking   Also called breakdancing, a dance of elaborate solo moves done to rap music.

deejay   The Jamaican predecessor to today's MC.

DJ   Also called a disc jockey, a person who plays and mixes music, creating new formulas and styles.

funk   A style of music popular in the 1970s, known for its repetitive and catchy bass beat.

graffiti   Writing or art done with spray paint, usually illegally, on public property.

hip hop   An African American cultural movement focused largely on rap music.

MC   Also called mic controller, a person who rhymes over the mix provided by the DJ.

mic   Microphone.

mixing   Combining two or more songs or song fragments; a unique way to create a new song.

patois   The dialect of a specific cultural group, here referring to the one spoken in the Caribbean.

producer   A person with both a creative and technical role in making a song in a studio.

rap   A musical form of rhymed storytelling accompanied by rhythmic, heavily synthesized music.

sampling   Inserting part of a track into another.

scratching   A technique of manually moving a record back and forth under the needle to make a scratching sound.

track   A recording of music.

For Further reading

Adam Sexton, ed. *Rap on Rap*. New York: Bantam Doubleday Dell, 1995.

Aptheker, Herbert. *Afro-American History—The Modern Era*. Secaucus, NJ: Citadel/Carol Publishing, 1992.

Beckman, Janette, and B. Adler. *Rap: Portraits and Lyrics of a Generation of Black Rockers*. New York: St. Martin's Press, 1991.

Cooper, Martha, and Henry Chalfant. *Subway Art*. London: Thames & Hudson, 1984.

Cross, Brian. *It's Not About a Salary: Rap, Race, and Resistance in Los Angeles*. New York: Verso, 1993.

Fernando, S.H., Jr. *The New Beats: Exploring the Music, Culture, and Attitudes of Hip-Hop*. London: Payback Press, 1995.

Goss, Linda, and Marian E. Barnes. *Talk That Talk*. New York: Touchstone/Simon & Schuster, 1989.

Hebdidge, Dick. *Cut 'N' Mix: Culture, Identity, and Caribbean Music*. London: Comedia, 1987.

Hughes, Langston. *The First Book of Jazz*. Hopewell, NJ: The Ecco Press, 1997.

Kebede, Ashenafi. *Roots of Black Music: The Vocal, Instrumental, and Dance Heritage of Africa and Black America*. Lawrenceville, NJ: Africa World Press,1995.

Palmer, Robert. *Deep Blues*. New York: Penguin, 1981.

Southern, Eileen. *The Music of Black Americans: A History*. 3rd ed. New York: W. W. Norton, 1997.

Suso, Foday Musa. *Jali Kunda: Griots of West Africa and Beyond*. Roslyn, NY: Ellipsis Arts, 1996.

Afrika Bambaataa and The SoulSonic Force. *Planet Rock*. Tommy Boy (1982).

Beastie Boys. *License to Ill*. Def Jam (1989).

Boogie Down Productions. *Edutainment*. Jive (1996).

Brand Nubian. *In God We Trust*. Elektra (1993).

James Brown. *20 All-Time Greatest Hits*. Polydor (1991).

Miles Davis. *The Columbia Years, 1955–1985*. Columbia (1988).

De La Soul. *3 Feet High and Rising*. Tommy Boy (1989).

Dr Dre. *The Chronic*. Death Row/Interscope (1994).

Missy "Misdemeanor" Elliott. *Supa Dupa Fly*. Elektra (1997).

Eric B and Rakim. *Paid in Full*. 4th & Broadway (1987).

The Fugees. *The Score*. Ruffhouse/Columbia (1995).

Gang Starr. *Daily Operation*. Chrysalis (1992).

Grandmaster Flash and the Furious Five. The Message. Sugar Hill Records (1981).

Lauryn Hill. *The Miseducation of Lauryn Hill*. Ruffhouse (1998).

Ice Cube. *Amerikkka's Most Wanted*. Priority (1990).

Jeru the Damaja. *Sun Rises in the East*. PGD (1994).

Robert Johnson. *The Complete Recordings*. Columbia/Legacy (1991).

Jungle Bros. *Done by the Forces of Nature*. Warner Bros. (1989).

LL Cool J. *Mama Said Knock You Out*. Def Jam (1991).

Bob Marley. *Legend*. Island (1984).

Nas. *Illmatic*. Columbia (1994).

The Notorious B.I.G. *Ready to Die*. Bad Boy (1994).

Parliament-Funkadelic. *Tear the Roof Off (1974–1980)*. PGD/Polygram (1993).

Public Enemy. *It Takes a Nation of Millions to Hold Us Back*. Def Jam (1988); *Fear of a Black Planet*. Def

Jam (1990).

Queen Latifah. *All Hail the Queen*. Tommy Boy (1989).

Run-D.M.C. *Run-D.M.C.* Profile (1984); *Raising Hell*. Profile (1986).

Gil Scott-Heron. *Evolution and Flashback*. BMG/ RCA Victor (1999).

KRS-One. *Return of the Boom Bap*. Jive (1993).

The Sugar Hill Gang. *Best of the Sugar Hill Gang*. Sugar Hill Records (1996).

A Tribe Called Quest. *People's Instinctive and the Paths of Rhythm*. Jive (1990), *Low End Theory*. Jive (1990).

2Pac. *All Eyez On Me*. Death Row (1996).

Muddy Waters. *The Best of Muddy Waters: The Millennium Collection*. UNI/MCA (1999).

Watts Prophets. *When the '90s Came*. PGD (1997).

Wu-Tang Clan. *Enter the Wu-Tang*. RCA (1993).

The X-Clan. *To the East Backwards*. 4th & Broadway (1990).

Various Artists. *Priceless Jazz: Priceless Jazz Sampler*. GRP (1997).

Various Artists. *Reggae Roots*. Island (1999).

Various Artists. *Yoruban Drums from Benin, West Africa*. Smithsonian Folkways (1996).

Videography

Style Wars (1983), directed by Henry Chalfant and Tony Silver.

WildStyle (1982), directed by Charlie Ahearn.

Index

Credits

Acknowledgments

God/Allah. My beloved teacher Philip S. Budin, who leads me from darkness into light. Thank you. My spiritual sisters Radha Zoulas and Debbie Hertzog. My beautiful mother, Mina Salahshourian. My amazing father, Davoud Ayazi-Hashjin. My brother, Ali Ayazi-Hashjin, and sister, Chanelle Massahood. My grandparents, Mohammad Javad Salahshourian, Ezat Rayani, Ahmad Ayazi-Hashjin, Nosrat Malakouti-Hashjin. Aunties Mahnoush, Mehrnoush, Manoush, Mahtab, and my cousins. My supportive friends Laurent Wiseman, Natalie Harland, Leon Sua, Avisha Chehrazi, Dominic Patton, James Araali-Kabyanga, Neil Melmoth, Lim and Lee Tan, Katherine & Tom Harrison, Johnathan Stone, and the whole of the Ealing community whom I grew up amongst and who remain a precious family to me. Love and thanks to companions Joe Omotesho, Jessica Peel, Franklin Massahood, Judith & Joanna Rodriguez, Veronica Whiteman, Mohsen Pourhashem, Jac Benson II, Vera, and Mo & Navid Ahmadzadeh.

About the Author

Sherry Ayazi-Hashjin is a graduate of Central Saint Martins College of Art & Design in London, England. She has represented cutting edge photographers and worked closely with some of today's contemporary musicians. She has also collaborated on projects at MTV and VH1 in research and then in production. Articles and stories have appeared in the following publications: *Blues and Soul, Wire, Touch, Jazz Express, Big Mouth, Living Large, Yush!, Represent, On the Go, One World,* and *The North American National Library of Poetry.*

Photo Credits

Cover photo, pp. 2, 8, 17, 19, 32, 33, 38, 39, 45, 46, 55, 56–57 by Ernest Paniccioli; pp. 4, 12, 15, 16, 21, 24, 26, 52 © AP/Wide World Photos; pp. 6, 34, 54 © CORBIS/Ernest Paniccioli; p. 10 © Clint Clemens/International Stock; pp. 18, 29 © Archive Photos; pp. 23, 43, 44 © CORBIS/UPI; p. 25 © CORBIS/Penguin; p. 27 © CORBIS/Gordon Parks; p. 28 © Arista Records, courtesy of the Schomburg Center, New York Public Library; p. 31 © CORBIS/Ronnie Wright; p. 36 by Oliver H. Rosenberg; p. 41© CORBIS/SIN-TEE-MAX; p. 42 © CORBIS/Steve Jennings; p. 47 © CORBIS/Mitch Gerber; p. 48 © CORBIS/John Bellisimo; p. 50 © CORBIS/Lynn Goldsmith; p. 51 © CORBIS/Grant leDuc; p. 53 © Reuters/Leonard Foeger/Archive Photos.

Text Credits

Page 22 from *The Middle Passage* by Tom Feelings. Copyright © 1995 by Tom Feelings. Used by permission of Dial Books for Young Readers, a division of Penguin Putnam Inc. P. 48 from Brian Cross, *It's Not About a Salary...;Rap, Race, and Resistance in Los Angeles.* Copyright © 1993 by Brian Cross. Reprinted by permission of Verso. All others used by permission.

Series Design

Laura Murawski

Layout

Oliver Halsman Rosenberg

Consulting Editors

Erin M. Hovanec and Erica Smith
Thanks to Sara Coppin, Production Editor, and David Chiu, Editorial Assistant.